SPACE ALIENS LEARN ECONOMICS

The Star Smile Squad

ISBN: 9798866049981
Imprint: Independently published

Cover design by: The Star Smile Squad
Library of Congress Control Number: 2018675309
Printed in the United States of America

A big thanks to the Star Smile Squad - my amazing wife alien and my two little aliens!

To my wife, thanks for using your logical laser beam brain to keep my wacky alien ideas in check!

Kids - You're the best! Thanks for adding your super imaginative ideas and out-of-this-world artistic skills to this book.

You're the coolest space family ever!

"We came from faraway planets to learn about Earth's weird ways. We found out that economics is actually quite easy and fun, even for the silliest of aliens!"

QUIBBLES AND QUACKY- INTERGALACTIC EXPLORERS

CONTENTS

OUR ADVENTURE BEGINS

Get ready to blast off on an intergalactic adventure! This isn't your typical trip among the stars though. Forget black holes and blazing comets, we're travelling across the universe to learn about economics!

Yes, you heard right - economics. Doesn't sound very exciting, does it?

Well, hold onto your jetpacks! You're about to discover how truly fun economics can be. No boring lectures here. Instead, join funny aliens like Quibbles, Quacky, Zigglesnap and Zazzleberry on their wacky adventures will take you zipping across the cosmos to peculiar planets like WhiffleWorld, CherryBerry and Zymalooza. You'll laugh out loud at their space jokes while picking up smart money lessons along the way.

Think you already know it all about coins and buying stuff? Think again! There are always new things to discover, even for the brainiest space cadets.

So, buckle up and get set to launch into the best kids' economics book this side of Jupiter.

CHAPTER 1: QUIBBLES AND QUACKY'S SAVINGS ADVENTURE

Once upon a time, in a faraway galaxy lived two alien siblings named Quibbles and Quacky. They were always by each other's side, travelling across the cosmos to explore exciting new worlds and having the most amazing adventures together.

Quibbles had fiery red skin and a large flashing yellow light on the top of his forehead that went round and round like a space lighthouse. He was quite naughty and sometimes got into trouble. But even when things went wrong, he always found a clever way out, as if his very own lucky star were shining down on him. He had a weird habit of jumping up and down on the spot when he got excited, like a little red bouncing ball.

Quacky, on the other hand, was a brainy and careful alien. She had tomato coloured skin like her brother, and she wore large, thick, dark glasses. A special thing about her was that her antennas wiggled when she was thinking about something unusual or difficult. She made sure their intergalactic voyages were as safe as possible, always looking after everyone and making sure they were happy. Her nickname was 'Triple-Check' as she always checked everything three times to make sure it was just right.

The pair went to school at the Interstellar Academy on their home planet of Quazar. The school looked like a shiny silver space fortress. It had metal walls that gleamed and shimmered and classrooms that were lit with neon light. The air smelled of intergalactic ink and stardust, while floating desks added a touch of magic to their studies.

The little aliens at the school were always giggling and laughing together, making the place feel really happy and fun. Sometimes the teachers could be heard telling off Quibbles for playing a mischievous prank like hiding a rotten Lunar Egg under his classmate's desk!

Their teacher, Mr Voltron was tall and skinny like a light blue beanstalk. His hair was like glow-in-the-dark spaghetti, shining in all sorts of wild colours. His voice was so loud that faraway alien species could hear him on the other side of the galaxy!

One day Mr Voltron had a big surprise for the class. "Put on your rocket boots, kids! Guess what? Today we're going to visit a completely new place. It's a planet called Earth! Earth has people who walk on just two legs. They're called 'Humans.' And listen to this: they use things called money to buy stuff! Yep, they don't get things for free like we do here on Quazar."

Not all the little aliens were sure about the trip to the strange sounding Planet Earth. Quacky's antennas wiggled, showing that she was thinking hard. "I really don't know about this, Quibbles," she said, her round red face looking worried. "Do you think these humans are friendly? I've triple-checked my Galactic Guide, but it doesn't say."

But Quibbles was really excited about the idea of visiting Earth. The little red alien bounced up and down, the light on his head flashing brightly. "Don't be a silly Space Squid, Quacky! Imagine all the incredible Earthling things we can discover. We'll be the first Quazarians to try their, what do they call it... pizza?" He sounded really thrilled but also a bit impatient.

Quacky was still feeling quite nervous, but smiling a bit she finally agreed, "Okay, let's do this. I'm in!"

And just like that, they hopped into their school space saucer, along with Mr Voltron and their fun-loving and noisy alien classmates. They fastened their seatbelts tightly and with a whoosh, they blasted off on their cosmic journey towards Earth. After zooming through space for a really long time, their spaceship finally landed in a bustling human town called Moneymore.

Moneymore was a crazy whirlwind of a town, chock-full of bizarre and interesting sights. The towering glass buildings stretched towards the sky like giant icicles. Humans scurried around, chatting in their odd, musical language. Yummy smells floated from rows of tempting and exotic food stalls. The Earthlings handed each other glittery coins in return for a whole bunch of treasures, from shiny bracelets that jingled like space-bells to silly star sunglasses that could make even a Giggle Gorgon giggle. Quibbles and Quacky were amazed at how different Earth was to their own planet.

Quibbles and Quacky decided to explore the colourful markets of Moneymore. Soon they stumbled upon a stall called Starburst Surprises which sold lots of different alien treasures. Quacky's antennae waggled as she spotted a large luminous pink space crystal, which Quibbles agreed would make a perfect gift for their mum.

As they gazed longingly at the dazzling crystal, a sudden burst of wind gusted through the bustling market. Poor Quacky's little red tentacles couldn't hold onto her precious space coins in the strong wind, and she gasped in shock as they slipped away. The coins spun and twirled through the air before vanishing into a nearby vortex hole.

They stood frozen, their eyes wide like saucers, unable to believe what had just happened. Their precious space money, which they had been saving up for so long, was now gone, lost in the depths of the unknown.

Mr. Voltron had seen what had just happened and went over to make sure they were okay. His spaghetti-like hair was glowing in warm, soothing colours, and his voice sounded kind. "Oops, it looks like you have lost your space coins. Remember, you always need to be careful with your money and keep it safe".

Quibbles, though feeling a bit sad, was too brave to stay downhearted for long. With a determined look on his face, he declared, "Well, every cloud of moon dust has a silver lining. Now I know that next time I'll need to store my space coins in a wallet for safe keeping."

Mr. Voltron raised an eyebrow. "Hmm, the problem with that though is you might leave your wallet somewhere by mistake, or it might get stolen," he warned, making them think twice.

But Quacky had an idea. 'Okay, then. I'll stash my coins in my cuddly Plutonian Piggy Bank. It's so adorable. It can squeal in twenty different alien languages and makes a really cute oinking noise every time you put money in. That way, I can't lose it, and it will be safe from thieves like the Sneaky Solarians!"

Mr. Voltron's hair changed to a pale green colour, which showed that he agreed. "Keeping your space coins in a piggy bank is good, Quacky. But what if you're on another planet? You see a yummy space cookie you want to buy. Oops! Your coins are all the way back home in your piggy bank! Plus, counting those shiny coins one by one might take ages!'"

He went on, "How about we upgrade from piggy banks, my dear little aliens? Ever heard of a REAL bank! They will guard your money like a three-headed Zorgon guards its babies, and you can simply peek at your phone to see how much savings you have. No need to play 'count-the-coins'!" Even better, the bank also gives you a little bit of extra money called 'interest' for keeping hold of your space coins!"

Quacky seemed puzzled, her red antennas wiggling. "But how do we pay for things if we don't have any money with us?" she asked, looking really confused.

I'll show you," winked Mr. Voltron. They tiptoed into a bustling store, watching with amazement as they saw Earthlings magically paying for stuff at the store counter by tapping either their phone or colourful plastic cards.

"So, we can use those cards and phones to pay for things too?" Quibbles exclaimed, sounding very impressed.

Mr. Voltron nodded, his grin spreading wider across his blue face, "Exactly! Just like the humans do!"

You mean to tell me that humans have figured out how to send money through thin air, but they still haven't invented a decent teleportation device?" Quacky joked. "Priorities, humans!

With the tick-tocking of the cosmic clock showing that is was nearly dinner time, Mr. Voltron herded Quibbles, Quacky, and all their alien friends back aboard the spaceship (once Quacky had tripled-checked that they had everything they needed for their voyage of course!). They zoomed back home through the inky night sky. As Earth was fading from sight, Quacky let out a happy sigh, her antenna bouncing. "Well, we may have lost our space coins, but learned how to keep our money safe too!" Quibbles added, cheerfully, "And Earth was fun! Now, let's save up for an adventure to Planet Zoombula!"

CHAPTER 2: COSMIC CHOICES ON PLANET CHERRYBERRY

On the famous planet of CherryBerry, there lived a happy family of fat, round, purple aliens called the Zozzles. They looked like bouncy jellybeans with big, shiny silver eyes that sparkled like tiny stars.

Dad Zigglesnap was quite a character, always busy inventing wacky gadgets and widgets. He would often mumble funny words, so focused on his work that he might even forget his own head if it weren't screwed on! But he always had time for a goodnight hug.

Zog, his son, shared his dad's curiosity. He loved tinkering with space junk and was always creating amazing new things. He was a bit messy, often leaving his latest inventions scattered about. But Zog and his dad were an awesome team, always working on their next big idea.

Zara, their daughter, really loved daydreaming about the stars! She'd gaze out her window at twinkling stars, imagining aliens and far-off worlds. She was so deep in spacey thoughts that she'd forget where she put her stuff. Like the time she found her missing sock in the cereal box. Or when she discovered her rocket pen had been behind her ear all along!

Mom, Zazzleberry, was super smart and as sharp as a supercomputer. She was always busy sorting things out, like making sure they had enough space pizza for dinner. She was the brainy one in the family, and sometimes felt like the sensible captain of a spaceship with a silly crew that only wanted to mess around.

One sunny day, the Zozzle family hopped into their spaceship for a fun little adventure. They were zooming off to Zymalooza, a magical planet where their old friend Bleepop had a really cool shop. Bleepop was a chubby, pink alien with green spots. His shop was like an enormous treasure chest. It was filled with awesome stuff from all over the galaxy.

They zoomed through space faster than a shooting star and arrived at Zymalooza in no time.. As soon as they landed, they couldn't believe their eyes. The planet was amazing beyond their wildest dreams. And guess what? Hidden in the big, tall mountains were secret space portals that could take you to far-away parts of Zymalooza or even to distant galaxies in less than a second!

They jumped into a nearby space portal. In a flash, they found themselves at Bleepop's shop, light-years away. "Ooh, let's get exploring!" chirped Zara excitedly. Inside the shop, there was a wild mix of space wonders, each more peculiar than the last. Boxes in all sorts of crazy shapes towered on the shelves. Out-of-this-world smells wafted from shiny silver jars and containers. The store was like a magic box of strange and amazing things.

Suddenly, Zog spotted a glinting object on one of the shelves. "Oh my stars, Dad! Look, it's a 'Galaxy Gadget-Kit!" The kit was packed full of all sorts of fun widgets and gismos. "Just imagine what I could make with this gadget kit, Dad," Zog went on, his imagination already whirring like a spaceship engine, "I could turn all our old space junk into marvellous new inventions. And look at this! It only costs one space coin.

Meanwhile, Zara spotted something. It was a glimmering globe that twinkled like a miniature universe. "Dad, it's a Star-Whisperer Sphere! It's like holding the entire universe in your hands! And it whispers amazing secrets about the stars and distant galaxies. Please can we please buy it, Dad? It's only two space coins!"

But Zazzleberry's face was scrunched up in worry, her purple skin looking a shade darker than usual. "Hold on, little astronauts,' I've been keeping an eye on our spaceship's energy levels on my special space-phone and our tank is running really low. Looks like we might be in trouble. Bleepop, do you happen to sell any space fuel in your store?'"

Bleepop grinned, rubbing his fat pink hands together. "Ah ha, you're in luck, Zazzleberry!" he exclaimed. "I have just the thing for you. I recommend 'Galactic Goo', the ultimate rocket fuel from beyond the stars! This slimy and stretchy fuel is fluorescent green, bubbles and fizzes with energy, and can launch even the heaviest spaceship into orbit. Plus, it smells like lime bubble-gum and leaves a sparkly trail of glitter. It's a steal at only three space coins!"

Zazzleberry looked relieved and nodded. "Bleepop, your Galactic Goo sounds like the answer to a space traveller's prayer! We'll take it."

"Can we get our cool toys as well as the space fuel?" asked Zog hopefully.

Zara chimed in. "Oh, pretty please, Dad! Can we get them too?"

Zigglesnap sighed. His face was kind and understanding. "I'm sorry, my little ones, but I don't think we can. There are so many amazing things we could buy with our space coins, right? Like Zero Gravity Books, or a Moon Candy Machine, or even a Star Gazer Telescope for seeing faraway places. But we only have so many space coins. This is what we call 'scarcity.' It means not having enough money for everything we want to buy."

"Like now, we've only got three space coins, but all the things we want from Bleepop's shop would cost six coins - one for the Galaxy Gadget-Kit, two for the Star-Whisperer Sphere, and three for the Galactic Goo spaceship fuel. We would need six coins to get everything we want, but unfortunately, we only have three. And in this universe, three doesn't make six."

He kneeled down to Zog and Zara's height, looking into their curious faces. "You see, my little aliens, everyone always would like more things than they can actually8 buy with their space coins. Scarcity means we can't have everything we want."

Little Zara raised her hand, just like in school. "But Dad, how do we decide? It's a bit like when we're at the intergalactic café and have to choose from the various flavours of space ice cream. They all look so tempting!"

Zigglesnap smiled warmly at his daughter. "I know it's hard, Zara, but remember this - every time you pick one thing, you're saying no to something else. This is what we call *'opportunity cost'*- where we make a *'choice'* and give up something in return."

"Opportunity cost?" Zara asked, sounding puzzled.

"That's right. If we spend our space coins on the toys you like, we won't have enough left for the Galactic Goo, which we need to fly back home. It's about making a choice. You pick the thing that brings you the most happiness or helps the most. Even if it means not having something else."

"So, it's like choosing between a giant-sized bucket of star-flavoured popcorn or a huge bottle of celestial cola," Zog exclaimed, starting to get the point his dad was making. "We can't have both, but we need to think about what will make us happiest in the end, right?"

"We understand, Dad," Zara finally said. "We need the Galactic Goo more than anything else we want right now. We don't want to be stuck here on Zymalooza! Let's fuel up. Then we can zoom back home to our own planet!"

From that day forward, their family became famous throughout the galaxy for being the smartest space travellers, known for their wise choices. They always remembered their lesson about scarcity, opportunity cost and choice—how to make smart decisions about what to buy. Especially when they only have so many precious space coins to spend.

CHAPTER 3: ZARA AND ZOG LEARN ABOUT UTILITY

One sunny morning, on the beautiful planet of Zymalooza, two little aliens named Zara and Zog woke up very excited about the new day ahead. Their home was a shiny, silver dome-shaped house that sat at the top of a hill like a giant space helmet. The best part? A huge telescope on the roof! One of their favourite hobbies was gazing through their telescope at the wonderful sights of Planet Zymalooza. They loved looking out on the forest of crystal trees around their house that shimmered green like precious emeralds. Down the hill, lay a lake, its waters a stunning shade of indigo. The lake twinkled as if it were filled with a thousand tiny diamonds, all dancing and playing in the water. On dark nights, they zoomed in on the shooting stars which blazed across pitch-black sky, dreaming of the faraway places they could visit one day.

That morning, Zara and Zog found themselves with nothing to do. They were on a school break and feeling as jumpy as a pair of restless space monkeys. They tried to find fun things to keep them busy, but everything seemed as dull as a cloudy day on Planet BoringBorg.

They had spent most of the morning arguing over small things like who got to eat the last piece of moon pie, or whose turn it was to feed their pet cyborg. "Zog, it's my turn to use the telescope today!" Zara said grumpily. "I want to see if I can spot the Andromeda galaxy."

"But you always get to choose which galaxy we look at!" Zog argued sulkily, his hands fidgeting with a piece of space junk he had been messing around with.

After a bit more bickering, Zara's eyes lit up with a bright idea. "Hey, Zog," she said, "let's go to the space café! It might be fun and it's definitely better than staying at home and squabbling all day."

So, off they went. They jumped into the nearest magic teleporter, and within seconds they had arrived at the space café, a few million light years away. The café was one of the coolest places in the universe. There were luminous lights flashing and floating jellyfish dec.orations that bobbed around as if they were dancing in zero gravity. It was like stepping into a cosmic disco! The walls were a canvas of funky graffiti, each piece telling a different story of legendary space adventures. The air was filled with the sound of little aliens chattering and giggling as they enjoyed their snacks.

They saw lots and lots of ice cream tubs in all sorts of colours. They had tempting names like Strawberry Supernova, Cosmic Crunch, and Starry Night Surprise. 'Wow, look at all this ice cream!' Zara shouted. Then she looked a bit sad. "But we only have one coin. That means we can only pick one kind, even though they all look super-yummy. That's a hard pick, huh."

Zog, who loved tinkering and making new things, said, "Let's try the Stella Swirl. It's the newest invention of a famous species of aliens called the Creamonauts. It's like they've captured a whole galaxy of delicious tastes in one ice cream!"

But Zara disagreed. "No way! I think we should get the Asteroid Fudge instead. I have heard that it's like exploring all the flavours of the cosmos with every bite!"

"Come on, Zara!", teased Zog. "Are your taste buds lost in outer space?"

Zara said back cheekily, "Lost in space? Well, listening to your dull ideas about ice cream is like being stuck on a boring asteroid, Zog".

Zara and Zog started arguing about which flavour to choose, their voices getting louder as they each tried to make the other see their point. They both talked at the same time, their words tumbling over each other, turning their friendly chat into a noisy argument that filled the whole café.

Just as Zara and Zog's quarrel was getting out of hand, they suddenly heard a voice they knew well. They were happy to see that their old friend Professor Zingling had just arrived at the space café. He was a quirky-looking old alien with wild pale blue hair, big black glasses, and a white scientist's coat. "What's wrong, my friends?" he asked helpfully.

"Oh, Professor Zingling," said Zara. "We are having a real ice cream emergency here! We can't decide which one to choose."

"Ah, I see. Can't pick an ice cream, eh? Just go for the one that makes you the happiest!" Professor Zingling suggested. "You know when you have a big gulp of refreshing comet juice on a super-hot day on Mercury? That's what grown-ups call 'utility.' But for us, it's like counting Happy Points."

The Professor made a floating hologram screen appear in the air. "Look, Zara and Zog! This is your Ice Cream Happy Point Guide. We've got Stellar Swirl, Asteroid Fudge, and Moon Rock Marshmallow. The numbers from one to ten tell you how much each of you likes each flavour. The more you like it the more Happy Points you get. Or if you want to use smarty-pants talk, the more 'utility' you get."

Ice Cream Happy Point Guide

· **Stellar Swirl:**

> o Zara's Happy Points: 6

> o Zog's Happy Points: 7

.· **Asteroid Fudge:**

> o Zara's Happy Points: 8

> o Zog's Happy Points: 6

· **Moon Rock Marshmallow:**

> o Zara's Happy Points: 9

> o Zog's Happy Points: 9

"So, let's think," said Professor Zingling. "Stellar Swirl gives you, Zara, 6 Happy Points because it's good but not your favourite. Zog, you get 7 because you like it more."

"And for Asteroid Fudge, Zara, you get 8 Happy Points because you love it! Zog, you think it's just okay, so you get 6 Happy Points."

"See?" Professor Zingling added, "It's completely fine that you each get your own number of Happy Points from the same ice cream!"

"I get it," Zara said, holding Zog's hand. "It's okay if I like one thing and you like another."

"Totally," Zog agreed, squeezing her hand back. "We all like different stuff, and that's cool."

"And Moon Rock Marshmallow?" Professor Zingling continued. "You both think it's the best and get a whopping 9 Happy Points! So that's the one to pick for the most happiness—or in other words as you'll learn when you're older, the highest 'utility.'"

Zara beamed, "So, we just choose what makes us happiest!"

Professor Zingling clapped his hands, and his laughter echoed around them. "You've got it! You're not just budding ice cream experts; you two are becoming real economics whizzes too!"

So, feeling very clever about spending their space coins so sensibly, they bought a gigantic scoop of Moon Rock Marshmallow to share. It was fluffy like a cloud and as sweet as the nectar from a Luna Lily. They found a comfy rock to sit on and began to eat, their tongues tingling with the cool sweetness.

As they enjoyed their yummy ice cream, they watched the sunset change colours like a magic rainbow in the sky. Zara and Zog kept thinking about what Professor Zingling had told them. Finally, Zara asked, 'Professor, how can we use this 'utility' idea in our everyday life?'"

"Great question, Zara!" he replied. "It's not just for picking ice cream, you know. Thinking about utility can help us decide all sorts of things!" He continued, "Let's say you're choosing a space pet—like a Fluffy Floggle or a Glittery Glibber. Think about which one you think is the cutest or which one makes you smile the most. Give each pet some Happy Points. Then pick the one with the most Happy Points, or to say another way, the one which gives you the most utility!"

"Or imagine this! You're at the Space Fair and you have two super fun rides to pick from: the Rocket Rollercoaster or the Starry Ferris Wheel. Which one is the most cool and exciting? The ride with the most Happy Points is the one you should go on! That way, you get the most happiness, and that's what we call 'utility' in big-kid talk!"

"Awesome! We'll keep that in mind. Thanks for the great lesson, Professor," said Zog.

Walking back home with their tummies filled with ice cream, Zara nudged Zog. "You know, Zog," she said, "I think we learned an important lesson today. We all like different stuff, and that's totally fine. And knowing our 'happy points' can help us make better choices, right?" Zog nodded, his face serious, and added,

"Yeah, whether we're picking ice cream or deciding on anything else, it's all about what gives us the biggest amount of utility."

That evening, when they got home to their futuristic house on the hill, they gazed at the night sky through their telescope. To their surprise, they spotted Professor Zingling soaring past in his spaceship. He looked down at them and smiled, proud of what they had learnt that day about economics.

CHAPTER 4: GRANDMA WIGGLYWILLOW'S BUDGETING ADVICE

Long, long ago, on a planet far from Earth, there lived a friendly and adventurous family of space aliens called the Wobblestars. They were small, slim, and banana-yellow, with pointy ears, friendly elf-like faces, and always looked happy. There were two little sisters, Wizzy and Wanda, and their clever space alien grandma, Wigglywillow.

The Wobblestar family lived on the unusual and colourful planet of Whiffleworld, where friendly aliens loved to hang out together, and everything was made of twinkling crystals that changed colours every day. Whiffleworld was known across the whole universe for its super-yummy space fruit.

Wizzy was a curious little alien who knew how to chat in Blibberish, Flibbertalk, and tons of other cool space languages. This made her the best buddy to travel with, as she could chat with all kinds of different creatures on their adventures. But Wizzy had one big wish: she really wanted to get a special magical machine, the 'Intergalactic Translator', so she could speak every alien language perfectly without making any mistakes.

Wanda was Wizzy's younger sister and best friend. She loved anything colourful or shiny and dreamed of one day starting her own super-cool space garden. Her plan was to fill her garden with all the amazing things she found on their adventures, like glowing moon rocks and peculiar little alien gnomes. But her biggest wish was to collect some extra-special Star Shimmer Crystals. She could just imagine how their twinkling light would turn her dream space garden into the most beautiful sight the universe had ever seen.

Their grandma, Wigglywillow, might be old and have lots of wrinkles, but she is also famous all over the planet for being incredibly clever and wise. She could whip up all sorts of amazing alien potions and magic spells, as if she had a never-ending book of secret recipes in her head. One day, Wanda's favourite rainbow-coloured Saturn Flower was looking tired and sad. But clever Grandma Wigglywillow made a potion, sprinkled it on the flower, and ta-da! It bloomed brighter than ever! She often brewed potions with weird side effects. One time she tried to create a spell to make their space veggies grow faster, but ended up with singing sprouts that would hum funny tunes whenever they were watered.

One sunny day, while the Wobblestars were out exploring a far-off planet, they found an unusual object hidden under a rock—a piggy bank! The two alien sisters, wanting to know more, asked their grandma what it was for. "You can use it to save your space money for later instead of spending it right away," Wigglywillow explained with a chuckle.

Little Wizzy squealed excitedly, "So it's like a cute little pink safe for our cosmic cash!" Wanda responded with a giggle, "Sounds like an oink-tastic way to protect our money!"

Wizzy blurted out, "It sounds a bit like a treasure hunt! We put our space coins away for a while, and later, we find a lovely surprise!" Wanda seemed a bit puzzled, "Why should we wait for later when we could just spend our money right now? Wouldn't that be way more fun?"

The kind grandma replied, "Well, it's like choosing between a little treat now or a big treat later. Imagine you want to buy a big, shiny-space-scooter that costs ten space coins, but your pocket money is only one space coin each week. If you spend all your pocket money every week on something naughty like a cosmic cupcake, you'll never be able to buy the space scooter. But if you are clever and save up your one space coin each week, after ten weeks, you'll have enough to afford it!"

Wizzy piped up, "Could saving up help me get my Intergalactic Translator?" Wanda chimed in, "And also my Star Shimmer Crystals?" Wigglywillow nodded, "Saving up is important, but you shouldn't save all your coins. Spend some for fun too! Balance is best—save some, spend some. That way you'll get what you want eventually and still have a nice time along the way."

The little pair wanted to listen to their grandma's advice and save their money. But as the week went by, they saw lots of yummy things they wanted to buy, like Alien Apple Pies and Star-Shaped Scones. Then one day, Zippy the ice-cream man showed up in his colourful truck. The smell of Moon Dust Mint and Strawberry Supernova ice cream was so good that it was really hard to not spend their coins.

Wigglywillow began to realise that her grandkids should learn more about how money works. So, she decided to take them on a magical trip to a far-off world called Coinia. On that distant planet, they visited a famous alien market and encountered all sorts of strange and fascinating creatures, each with their own special ways of spending and saving their money.

First off, they ran into the Thriftlings. With their big red claws and shiny black eyes, these crab-like aliens clung tight to their space coins, clutching them as if they were rare lunar gems. It was very unusual for them to buy anything at all, as they were so careful to hang on to their coins. Luckily, Wizzy knew the Thriftlings' slow and careful language, so she was able to talk with them.

The stern-faced Thriftlings snapped their pointy red claws as they talked. "Counting our lovely coins and stacking them into tall towers is our favourite hobby!" they declared. But Wizzy found out that the Thriftlings had completely forgotten how to have a good time. Because they saved too much, they didn't get to do all the fun activities in life like Space Bowling and Kosmic Karaoke.

"They are like real-life calculators!" Wizzy remarked, watching the Thriftlings. "Yeah, but they seem to have lost their fun button," Wanda replied, noting their glum faces. She thought about how quickly she could get her Galactic Translator if she saved up all her money like they did. But seeing how boring they were made her think that she didn't want to be like them.

Then they met the Glitzgrabs, big, orange bird-like creatures who spent their coins faster than a speeding space rocket. They rushed from one shiny treasure to the next, their big, greedy eyes wide with excitement. They loved shopping for new and fun things like Meteorite Marbles or Intergalactic Sticker Sets. But just like a sparkly bubble that pops all too soon, their interest in their new toys disappeared quickly, and they were always on the lookout for the next cool thing to buy. Wanda laughed, wondering if they had zero-gravity coins, as they seemed to float right out of their scaly claws!

"These Glitzgrabs are like crazy kids in a candy store!" Wizzy chuckled in amazement.

Wanda looked doubtful. She noticed how they quickly ran out of coins when they really needed them and remembered that it was important to save up for her Star Shimmer Crystals.

Unfortunately, Wizzy accidentally mixed up her Glitzgrab words. Instead of asking about why they were spending their money so quickly, she ended up challenging one to a race! The speedy Glitzgrab was actually quite amused, and it turned into a fun chase around Coinia Market!

Finally, they met the Balanced Creatures, who swung from one colourful stall to another with their long, furry arms and curly tails. Their grinning, monkey-like faces lit up with glee whenever they found a bargain. Unlike the Thriftlings who hoarded every space coin, or the Glitzgrabs who spent everything right away, the Balanced Creatures had a smarter plan. They carefully considered when to use their coins to buy things they really fancied and when to save them for something special.

Wizzy said, "Meeting the Balanced Creatures taught us something important; we should spend some of our money on fun stuff now but also remember to save some too."

Wanda nodded her head, "You're right. Let's buy one tasty Cosmic Cupcake and one scoop of cool Interstellar Ice Cream now and save the rest."

After weeks of saving their shiny space coins, they realized that they had enough money for whatever their hearts desired. Wizzy jumped up and down, shouting cheerfully, "Yippee! I can buy my amazing Intergalactic Translator!" Wanda danced around with glee, joining in cheerfully, "And I can get my gorgeous Star Shimmer Crystals!" They'd made their dreams come true, all while enjoying some really tasty snacks in the meantime.

Looking happy, Wizzy declared, "Wanda, we've done it! We've become 'Budget-nauts!'" Chuckling, Wanda replied, "Astronauts who know how to budget? That's absolutely out-of-this-world."

To celebrate their adventure, they enjoyed an amazing meal of space fruit back home on Whiffleworld. Grandma Wigglywillow looked at them with a knowing smile and said, 'You two learned something important today. Having fun now is great, but saving for later is also a good idea.'

She pulled a tiny box from her pocket and opened it. Inside were two glowing seeds. "These are Future Seeds. If you plant them in your space garden, they'll grow into something really cool when you need it. Just like saving your money, these seeds are a treasure for later."

The two little aliens gave their clever grandma a big hug, then went into their space garden to plant the Future Seeds. Afterward, they gazed up at the twinkling stars, thrilled about all the future adventures waiting for them. Wizzy turned to Wanda and said, "Just think, these seeds are like our dreams. With a little time and care, who knows what they'll grow into!'"

CHAPTER 5: TRADING ON PLANET KAZUMARI

It was another chilled and cheerful day on the planet of Kazumari. Dreamy, fluffy clouds drifted through the sky, and everything was peaceful and calm. There was entrancing music all around, and the aliens who lived there, called the Kazumarians, loved to relax on big, soft sofas, listening to melodic tunes. They floated happily around, gliding from one place to another as if they were weightless.

Two aliens called Kuki and Keeko lived on Kazumari with their mum and dad. Kuki was funny and full of energy. She had blue skin like the deep ocean waves and always wore a pink, glittery hat that sparkled on her head. When she laughed at her funny stories, her face turned really blue, and her hat twinkled and shimmered a cool, bubblegum colour. Her biggest dream? To fill a book with her funniest space jokes and share it with friends across the universe.

Keeko, Kuki's brother, also had bright blue skin, with wild, spiky hair that looked like zigzag lightning bolts. Whenever his favourite game, Space-Ball, was on CosmoCast TV, he'd dance around like a spinning planet. His biggest dream was to become the champion of the Stellaxon Space-Ball Tournament.

One day they decided to blast off in their spaceship and visit the faraway alien city of Nebula Wharf. "Wow, look at this city, Keeko!" Kuki exclaimed, pointing out of the spaceship's window as they touched down. The tall buildings reached up to the sky, shining like giant ice crystals. Nebula Wharf was teeming with different types of weird and wonderful aliens bustling around on the busy streets. The gentle buzz of spaceships zooming around filled the air. Bright, colourful lights danced on the river, making it twinkle under the starry night sky.

The two little aliens jumped out of the spaceship and went for a walk, meeting lots of rather interesting aliens along the way. First, they met the Cosmic Consumers, who could usually be found squandering their space coins in the malls of Nebula Wharf. These chubby, pink creatures had greedy, pudgy-looking faces and silly, squeaky voices, and they were always excited about trying new things. "See this chattering Plutonian Parrot? We love buying fun things like this," giggled a fat little Cosmic Consumer.

Next, they met some Planetary Producers, slim pale grey-coloured aliens with big grey eyes and even bigger brains. They showed the two little aliens around their shop, buzzing with enthusiasm about the new things they had to sell. One of the Producers grinned, pointing to a huge pile of Tootletron Teddy bears. "See those? We made 'em! That's what we do – make and sell goods and services that Cosmic Consumers like to buy. It's always a guessing game, figuring out what they'll want next."

Keeko, looking puzzled, scratched his head. 'What do you mean by "goods?"' he politely asked the pale blue aliens. 'Goods are things that we can touch and use,' one of the Planetary Producers replied. 'They're like toys that you play with, such as Lunar Lego or Comet Cube Puzzles, or things that you eat like Moon Meatballs or Solar Serpent Steak. You can buy them in stores or online to make your lives more fun and exciting.' He pointed a thin grey finger to a nearby holographic TV screen, which was showing ads for different kinds of bizarre alien goods:

• Martian Mind Reader: Imagine being able to know what your alien friends are thinking! With our Martian Mind Reader, that's possible! You just stick it on your forehead, and like magic, you can hear their thoughts. No more guessing games. For only four space coins, you can unlock the secrets of their mind.

• UFO Detector: This fun gadget tells you when UFOs are nearby! It glows and beeps when there's an alien around. It even comes with a cool guide that explains different kinds of UFOs, like glowing Orbitrons or saucer-shaped SkySkippers! You can get it for just six space coins.

• Alien Language Translator: This clever little widget can turn any alien language into English! Great for chatting with different creatures, solving secret messages, and learning new languages. It's super easy to use and comes with nifty earbuds that look like little alien antennas! This is on sale for only five space coins.

"Those goods do sound really cool", said Kuki. "But it's such a shame we can't afford them, we only have two space coins between us", she sighed, looking sadly into her silver purse.

Keeko asked excitedly, "Hold on, what about this thing called services? Can you tell us more?"

"Services are fun or useful things that other aliens do to help you out," the Planetary Producer explained. "You can't see or hold them like toys, but they sure do make life better! Like when you go to a Stella Spa to relax in a refreshing pool of glowing liquid stardust, or when you call in your shiny Robo-Cleaner, with its flashing lights and whirling tools, to make your messy moon base neat and tidy again."

The Planetary Producer then pointed to the hologram TV screen, which was now showing adverts for a range of peculiar alien services:

.• Interplanetary Delivery Service: Got a parcel for another planet? No problem! It'll get there quicker than the speed of light in one of our special turbo-charged rockets, zooming across the cosmos in no time! Only four space coins for each parcel.

• Galactic Getaway Guides: Fancy a break that's out of this world? Imagine hiking in moon craters, floating in zero gravity, or surfing on solar waves. All these unforgettable adventures are just six space coins away.

• Alien Pet Care: Got an alien pet? Whether it's slimy or fluffy, we cater to all. Snotsnails, Astrohamsters, you name it! We feed them, groom them, and take them for walks. We'll keep your pet over-the-moon happy for just five space coins.

"Those services are totally awesome," Kuki exclaimed, clapping her hands. But then her smile faded a bit. "Too bad we don't have enough money for them," she murmured sadly. "I really wish we had brought more than two space coins on our trip. Everything here in Nebula Wharf costs an arm and a tentacle!"

The Planetary Producer held up a shiny coin, his thumb running over it. "You see, these gadgets do cost a few space coins, and that's what we call their 'price,'" he explained. "The price tells us how many space coins we need to trade for goods and services."

"And you know what?" he said kindly. "Sometimes the price can be quite high. It can seem unfair and make us feel sad. But that's just how the universe works."

The Planetary Producer went on explaining to Kuki and Keeko "Okay, just think for a moment. We need to spend our own coins on things like buying materials and paying our alien workers to make the goods and services. Even the fuel for the spaceship that brings them here costs money. And the more special a thing is to people, the more they are willing to spend their hard-earned space

SPACE ALIENS LEARN ECONOMICS

coins on it. That's why prices can be a bit high sometimes."

Suddenly, Keeko had a brainwave. "Hey, what if we invent something to sell, just like the Producers?" he said, smiling hopefully. Kuki paused, imagining the huge pile of shiny space coins they could earn. A big grin spread across her face. "Keeko, that's a super-duper idea!" she agreed.

So, the two alien friends put their heads together, or antennas, or whatever they had, and eventually managed to invent a really brilliant gadget—the Snack-O-Matic! Kuki pushed a big green button on the Snack-O-Matic, and a Star Cake popped out. "Hey, Keeko, try this!" she called out excitedly. Keeko took a big bite, his face lighting up in delight. "These Star Cakes taste yummy. Which button makes the Comet Croissants?"

Finding customers was harder than they thought. At first, their food stand seemed about as popular as a black hole at a star party. But they didn't give up. Instead, they put on a live entertainment show: Kuki told her wackiest alien-style jokes while Keeko invited passersby to quick games of Space-Ball. Before long, a crowd of eager aliens had gathered.

Their nifty machine became super popular all around the galaxy. One alien told another, and before they knew it, Kuki and Keeko found themselves with a mountain of shiny space coins from Snack-O-Matic sales. They could finally enjoy the luxuries of Nebula Wharf, from floaty zero-gravity parks to high-speed sonic scooters. But the best part? They weren't just watching the fun; they were part of the action.

Kuki gave Keeko a friendly nudge. "We kept going, even when it was tough. Look at us now!" Keeko laughed and bobbed up and down, like a floating asteroid. "Totally, Kuki! We make tasty snacks, others enjoy eating them, and we get more space coins. It's like the best and cleverest game ever!"

CHAPTER 6: SUPPLY AND DEMAND AND LUNAR LIMES

Kuki and Keeko were at home on Planet Kazumari one day. "My little darlings, I need you to go to the market to buy some ingredients for dinner," said their kind alien mum. "Make sure you get some purple yogurt, sparkling starfruit, and galaxy nuts," she said, handing them a list.

Kuki teased her brother, "Race you to the marketplace, Keeko!" It was like the start of a Space-Ball game for Keeko, who zoomed off into the distance, his hair flashing like lightning.

As the pair of alien friends dashed happily around the market, chattering and laughing together, they couldn't help but notice that some food items were much more expensive than others. They saw a tiny bag of fat juicy alien mushrooms that cost ten whole space coins, while a huge bag of slimy space slugs was just one space coin.

Kuki said laughing, "Gosh! These mushrooms must be super tasty! Hehehe HooHooHoo!" Her weird giggle was so funny, it made everyone at the busy market laugh too. Kuki pointed at the mushrooms. "Why do they cost so much, while this big bag of space slugs is so cheap?"

Behind his market stall, the friendly seller leaned down to the little aliens' level, chuckled, and said, "Well, my young star travellers, it's all about something called 'supply and demand.'"

Keeko asked curiously, "What's this 'supply and demand' thing you're talking about? I have never heard of that before!"

"Well, demand is how much buyers want something and how many space coins they're willing to give for it," said the seller.

"And supply is about how much of that thing we sellers have and how many coins we think we could get for it."

"You see, the mushrooms are very popular because they taste so yummy. They have a mouthwatering flavor that many aliens can't resist. Plus, they're packed with all sorts of ingredients that are good for your health. That's why they're in high demand and cost a lot of space coins."

Keeko was impressed, "Amazing, they're the Space-Ball champions of the food world—popular and healthy too!"

"That's exactly right," said the seller, with a friendly grin. "Alien Mushrooms also cost more because they are very rare. They only grow in certain places in the far corners of Planet Kazumari, under a particular type of Moonbeam tree, and only at special times of the year, like around the time of the Galuxura Festival. So, there aren't many of these mushrooms around, or in other words, supply is low. That's also why you need to spend a lot of space coins just to get a small little bag."

Keeko, bringing the topic back to his favorite pastime, said, "So, the more valuable and rarer something is, the more it costs. Just like with Space-Ball game tickets during the Stellaxon Superbowl!" They're always in high demand, and the supply is limited, which is why they are so crazy expensive.

"Right," said the seller, nodding wisely. "On the other hand, the less valuable and more common something is, the fewer space coins it costs."

"So, you mean like those slimy space slugs over there?" said Kuki. "That's just it," said the seller. "They're not very popular because they're greasy and oily and not very tasty. So, demand for slugs is low. Also, space slugs are very common because they can easily survive in many different places, and they can have lots of babies very quickly. This means there are a lot of them around. So, .the supply of slugs is high too." The two friends looked at the slugs with dislike, wrinkling their noses at the sight of the disgusting grey creatures.

"Aha!" yelled Kuki, her deep blue face lighting up like a supernova as the idea started to make sense. "I totally get it now! So, supply and demand work like a seesaw we play on..." She began to move her hands in opposite directions, just like how a seesaw moves. "When a lot of people want something—the demand—one side goes up, and so does the price. But if there's a lot of that thing around—the supply—that's like the other side of the seesaw. It pushes the price down."

"You got it!" The seller beamed at them, handing them each a bag of yummy alien fruit. "Here, try these juicy star apples. They're a special present from me." After eating their tasty gifts, the little aliens left the marketplace, feeling very happy indeed. They knew they had learned something important."

"Hey, Keeko, I have a fab idea!" said Kuki, looking very excited. "What if we started our own alien fruit stand? We could sell only fruit with high demand and low supply, so we can charge big space bucks for them!"

"Hey, you are a genius!" exclaimed Keeko, jumping up and down with glee. "We could sell the juiciest, sweetest, and most delicious fruit in the galaxy!" We will be rich!"

So off they went, whizzing through the cosmos in their flying saucer, searching all over the galaxy for the perfect space fruit. Despite visiting hundreds of planets, they just couldn't find the right one.

In time, they found an amazing type of fruit called Zesty Zetaberries on a nearby planet called Citrusia. They were sweet and juicy, perfect! But after setting up their stand, they discovered the Zetaberries caused silly orange spots on their customers' faces when they ate them, which made them very annoyed indeed. They needed a new fruit quickly!"

Just as they were about to give up and go home to their own planet, they found a small, round fruit with a shiny green skin and a sour and refreshing taste. It was called a Lunar Lime. It felt cool and a little squishy. When they cut it open, a sharp candy-like smell filled the air.

They each tried a chunky piece and a smile spread across their faces as the tangy taste tickled their tongues. "This is it, Kuki!" Keeko said, sounding as thrilled as if he'd found an ancient treasure chest full of golden Nebula Eggs. "I can already see all the aliens lining up to taste these!" They knew that they had found something amazing which would be in high demand. They could see supply would be low too, as Lunar Limes only grew on very rainy planets like Citrusia. Their plan was to load up their spaceship with every Lunar Lime they could find. Their new fruit stand was going to make them a fortune beyond their wildest dreams!

"But the Lunar Limes were guarded by a ferocious Star Giant named Supernova Stan. Our alien pals had to tiptoe and be super quiet to grab those special limes without waking him up! With each gentle step, they moved closer to the precious fruit, their hearts pounding. While the giant kept on snoring peacefully, they safely scurried away. They were so happy!

Next, they set up their own mini-website and started selling their fruit. At first, not many aliens made orders. It was a bit quiet. Then, Kuki had a bright idea, 'Let's give away some free purple yogurt with every Lunar Lime,' she suggested. Keeko agreed. Soon, their idea became a big hit. Aliens from galaxies near and far wanted to taste the yummy Lunar Limes and the cool purple yogurt. Their website buzzed with orders, earning the little aliens more and more space money.

As Kuki and Keeko headed back to their home planet, Kazumari, they made a quick stop at the Moon Market. They had lots of silver space coins jingling in their pockets, and they wanted to buy some special alien food for their family. Remembering what they learned about supply and demand, they chose treats that were yummy but also a great deal! They avoided the overpriced Moonberries and instead got a huge bag of StarPops, which were just as delicious but way cheaper. When they zoomed back home, their mum's eyes nearly popped out of her head! 'You two are not only amazing intergalactic explorers, you're super-smart shoppers too!'"

.

CHAPTER 7: THE ECO-HEROES OF WHIFFLEWORLD

Wizzy and Wanda's home in Whiffleworld was the coolest cosmic hangout you could ever imagine! The walls were covered in glittering lights and colorful disco balls that dangled from the ceiling, making the room shimmer and sparkle like the inside of a magical alien cave. And oh, the furniture? It was like something straight out of a space explorer's dream, made with funky otherworldly shapes and cushioned with soft, fluffy pillows like marshmallows.

The Whiffleworld aliens were not only super friendly, but they were also famous for being brilliant musicians! There were all kinds of weird musical instruments and gadgets lying around the house, from galactic guitars to space bongo drums.

One day, our musical duo was lounging lazily on their colourful bean bag chairs while listening to Martian music. Sitting up, Wanda turned towards Wizzy and said, 'Have you ever heard of a musical instrument called a Whistlewood?' her fingers dancing along to the alien tune as if she were playing an invisible keyboard.

'It's made from these super-special Whiffleworld trees, and oh boy, it has such an amazing, magical sound,' said Wanda, excitedly.

'Wow, that does sound like a cool instrument,' said Wizzy, with a curious look on her face. 'Please, tell me more!'

'The branches are hollowed out and then joined together to make a long, twisty, brown tube. It looks like a moon snake, ready to charm you with its melodies,' said Wanda, describing the wind instrument. 'To play the Whistlewood, you have to blow into one end and then move your fingers up and down the tube to create different notes,' she added.

'That's exactly what we need to create our new bestselling song! Imagine the Whistlewood blending with the sweet sound of our galactic guitars!' Wizzy exclaimed, jumping off her bean bag chair. 'Let's go and buy one right away!' So, they set off to the nearby forest called Florala Nexus, where there was a special musical instrument shop."

Eventually, they arrived at Florala Nexus Forest. The trees were like towering old green giants, their leaves twinkling like emeralds. The air smelled sugary like the pink clouds of Planet Sweetalia, and the extraterrestrial birds tweeted a happy tune.

"Yikes, Wizzy, this forest is incredible!" said Wanda, admiringly.

"Yeah, it's pretty cool," agreed Wizzy.

"I really hope we find some sparkly space rocks here for my space garden!" said Wanda, her eyes sweeping wishfully across the forest floor.

As they were wandering through the forest, they heard a loud and horrible noise like a swarm of angry bees. They followed the nasty sound and found a bunch of mean, ugly aliens chopping down trees with huge scary saws. These were the dreaded Beastly Buzzcutters. They had green eyes and orange, scaly skin, kind of like a Cinder Lizard.

With sparks flying, the Buzzcutters' roaring saws tore through the ancient trees. Wizzy and Wanda marched bravely up to the terrible creatures.

"Stop!" Wizzy cried out, her voice echoing through the clearing. "Why are you cutting down these beautiful old trees?"

The Buzzcutters ignored the pair completely. They just kept hacking away in silence, evil smirks stretching across their scaly faces. The giant trees crashed down around them, one after another.

Shaking their heads in sadness and disbelief, Wizzy and Wanda continued deeper into the forest. Eventually, they stumbled upon three peculiar-looking aliens. The first alien, named Verdora, had an elegant, slender, green body, and her head was shaped like a leaf. "Hello, friends," said Verdora. As she spoke, a small bird with bright, luminous feathers fluttered down and landed on her leaf-shaped head. "See this little guy? He's looking for a tree to call home. But if the trees are gone, where will he go?" A small, sad tear trickled down her beautiful green face. The bird chirped back and flew away.

The second alien, who said her name was Fluffy, was a cloud-like creature who floated gracefully through the forest. Fluffy drifted over to a tree and gently touched its bark. "This tree is like a superhero for our planet. Watch this!" Fluffy let out a puff of air, and the tree seemed to shimmer as if it were 'breathing in' the air. "See? Trees are like nature's vacuum cleaners; they suck up the nasty stuff in the air called greenhouse gases." Fluffy's cloud body shrank and turned darker as she floated away, looking really sad.

Sprout, the third alien, was very friendly and honest, with a big blue eye on his forehead that blinked with an otherworldly glow. Sprout's big blue eye flashed, and suddenly a holographic image of a space farm appeared in the air. "Take a look here. This is Farmer AstroAlf's moon vegetable farm!" Sprout then erased the trees from the hologram. "Now, watch what happens when the trees are gone." The soil turned grey, and the moon vegetables wilted. "See? No trees, no yummy moon veggies."

Wizzy and Wanda ventured deeper into Florala Nexus Forest, still eager to find the perfect Whistlewood instrument. They stumbled upon a shop nestled amidst the tall green trees. The shop was filled with all kinds of weird and wonderful Whistlewoods. Some had natural, leafy patterns carved into them, others had twisty shapes, and a few were even covered in glimmering stones.

The shopkeeper was a spooky elf-like alien named Sneakynose. With shifty eyes, pointy ears, and a sly grin, something about him was very creepy indeed. The alien duo noticed that all the Whistlewoods cost just one space coin, making them curious.

Wizzy asked Sneakynose warily, "Why do they only cost one space coin, usually they are more expensive than that?"

"I got them at a special low price from my best, best friends, the Beastly Buzzcutters!", replied Sneakynose with a dastardly chuckle.

Wanda looked worried and said, "I think these cheap instruments might be bad for our forests if they're made from trees cut down by the evil Buzzcutters. Let's pick a different store to buy from."

The two little aliens wandered hopefully around Florala Nexus until they eventually found another music store. This time, a cheerful, avocado-green shopkeeper named Sparklebeam greeted them warmly. She proudly showed them around her little shop, which had an unusual and interesting range of beautiful Whistlewoods neatly displayed on the shelves.

Wizzy and Wanda saw that the Whistlewoods in Sparklebeam's shop were a little more expensive, costing three space coins each instead of just one at Sneakynose's place.

Sparklebeam explained honestly, "The musical instruments in my shop may cost a bit more, but they are made by very good-hearted aliens called the EcoSavers. Every time they cut down a tree to make a Whistlewood, they plant two more!" Sparklebeam paused and looked seriously at Wizzy and Wanda. "You know, in our shop, we believe in something called Fair Trade. That's like making sure when you buy something, you're not just getting a cool thing for yourself; you're also making sure all plants and creatures are treated kindly."

Sparklebeam leaned a little closer and added, "Your space coins have power. They can either help save our forests or let them be harmed. So, choosing where to shop isn't just a small choice—it's a way to be a hero for our planet."

Wizzy and Wanda nodded, knowing their choices about how to spend their money were really important for the whole of Whiffleworld.

They handed over three shiny coins each and put their new purchases safely in their pockets. They were happy to pay a bit more in Sparklebeam's shop, knowing that each coin was like planting a new seed of hope in the forest!

Soon Wizzy and Wanda got back home and started making cool new music with their Whistlewoods. As the music flowed, they smiled, knowing they had made a choice that protected their environment. They realized that when you spend your space coins wisely, it makes you happy. And guess what? It makes the whole planet smile too!

THE LAST STAR OUR SPACE MAP

Hey, little alien explorers! We're taking a break and parking out spaceship for now, but learning economics stays exciting!

Our buddies Quibbles, Quacky, Zara, Zog, Keeko, Suzi, Wanda, and Wizzy taught us economics is for everyone. It helps us make smart choices, from ice cream to saving the Earth.

Little choices make big waves! As you grow big, you'll use this knowledge in awesome ways.

Our story pauses, but your adventure's just kicking off! Dream big, the future's yours to shape!

WHO ARE THE STAR SMILE SQUAD?

Join the Star Smile Squad! We're setting off on a super cool space adventure to explore the fun world of economics!

Every awesome team has its heroes. Mummy Alien makes sure all our big ideas stay on track. Sister Alien helps kids at school, making sure learning is always fun. And our two little aliens? They sprinkle their magic all over this book with their crazy ideas and drawings.

Now, let's talk about Daddy Alien. He's like a superhero of economics ! He's been doing this for twenty years and has worked on some really big jobs in the UK. When he talks about economics in this book, you know you're learning from one of the best!

Printed in Great Britain
by Amazon

31323002R00029